This book is dedicated to my mom,
who, as Marietta's father did for her,
opened my eyes to the wonder of creating and being an artist.

atheneum

ATHENEUM BOOKS FOR YOUNG READERS
An imprint of Simon & Schuster Children's Publishing Division
1230 Avenue of the Americas, New York, New York 10020
Copyright © 2020 by Evan Turk
All rights reserved, including the right of reproduction in whole or in part in any form.
ATHENEUM BOOKS FOR YOUNG READERS is a registered trademark of Simon & Schuster, Inc.
Atheneum logo is a trademark of Simon & Schuster, Inc.
For information about special discounts for bulk purchases, please contact
Simon & Schuster Special Sales at 1-866-506-1949 or business@simonandschuster.com.
The Simon & Schuster Speakers Bureau can bring authors to your live event.
For more information or to book an event, contact the Simon & Schuster Speakers Bureau
at 1-866-248-3049 or visit our website at www.simonspeakers.com.
Book design by Lauren Rille
The text for this book was set in IM Fell.
The illustrations for this book were rendered in watercolor, colored pencil, oil pastel,
and gold gouache on tan paper.
Manufactured in China
0520 SCP
First Edition
10 9 8 7 6 5 4 3 2 1
CIP data for this book is available from the Library of Congress.
ISBN 978-1-5344-1034-3
ISBN 978-1-5344-1035-0 (eBook)

Evan Turk

A Thousand Glass Flowers

*Marietta Barovier and the
Invention of the Rosetta Bead*

atheneum

Atheneum Books for Young Readers · *New York London Toronto Sydney New Delhi*

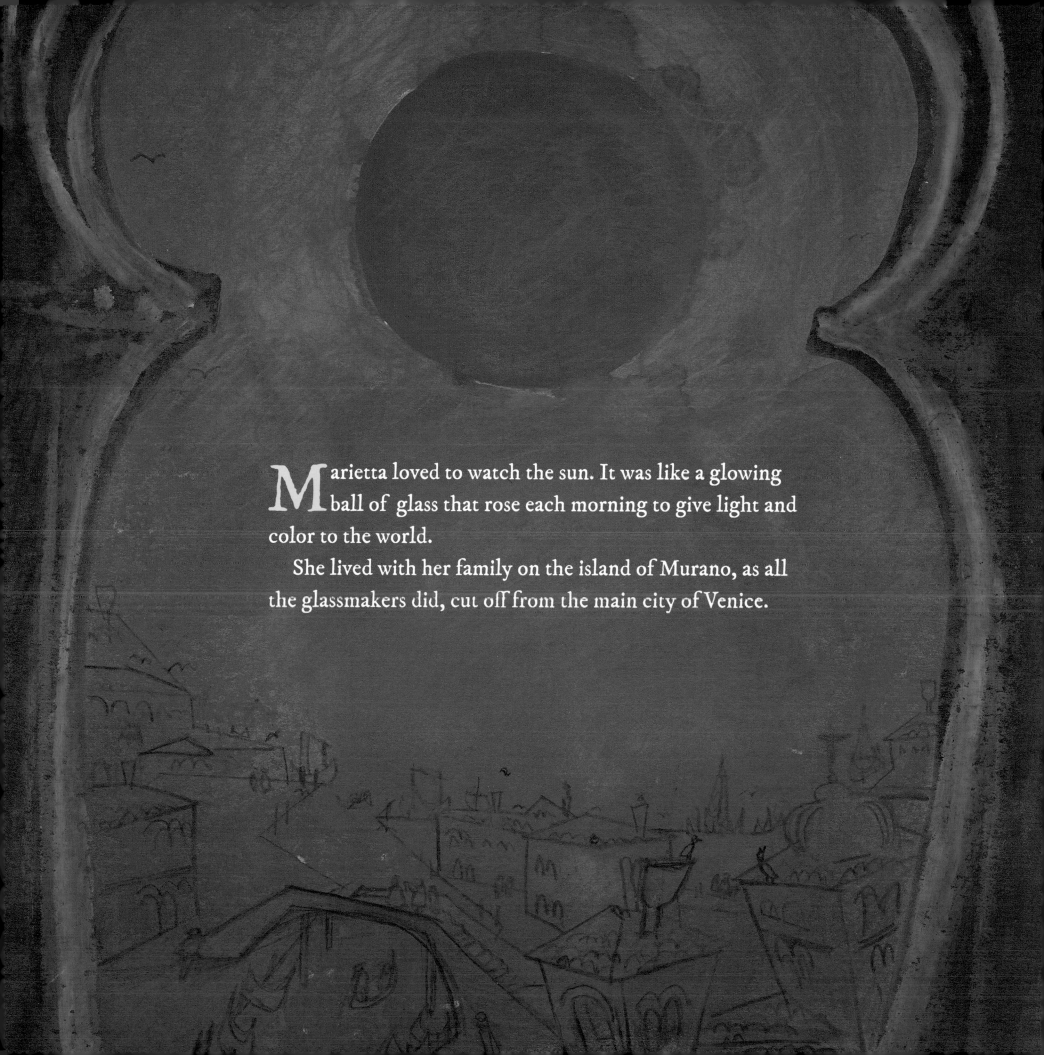

Marietta loved to watch the sun. It was like a glowing ball of glass that rose each morning to give light and color to the world.

She lived with her family on the island of Murano, as all the glassmakers did, cut off from the main city of Venice.

Her father, Angelo Barovier, was a true *maestro*, a master of glass. He performed miracles with it, turning the molten sand into elegant forms as clear as water, as white as milk, or as richly colored as precious stones.

Marietta dreamed of creating glass too, but glass was men's work. So while her brothers assisted their father with the blazing hot fires of the furnace, she stayed at home.

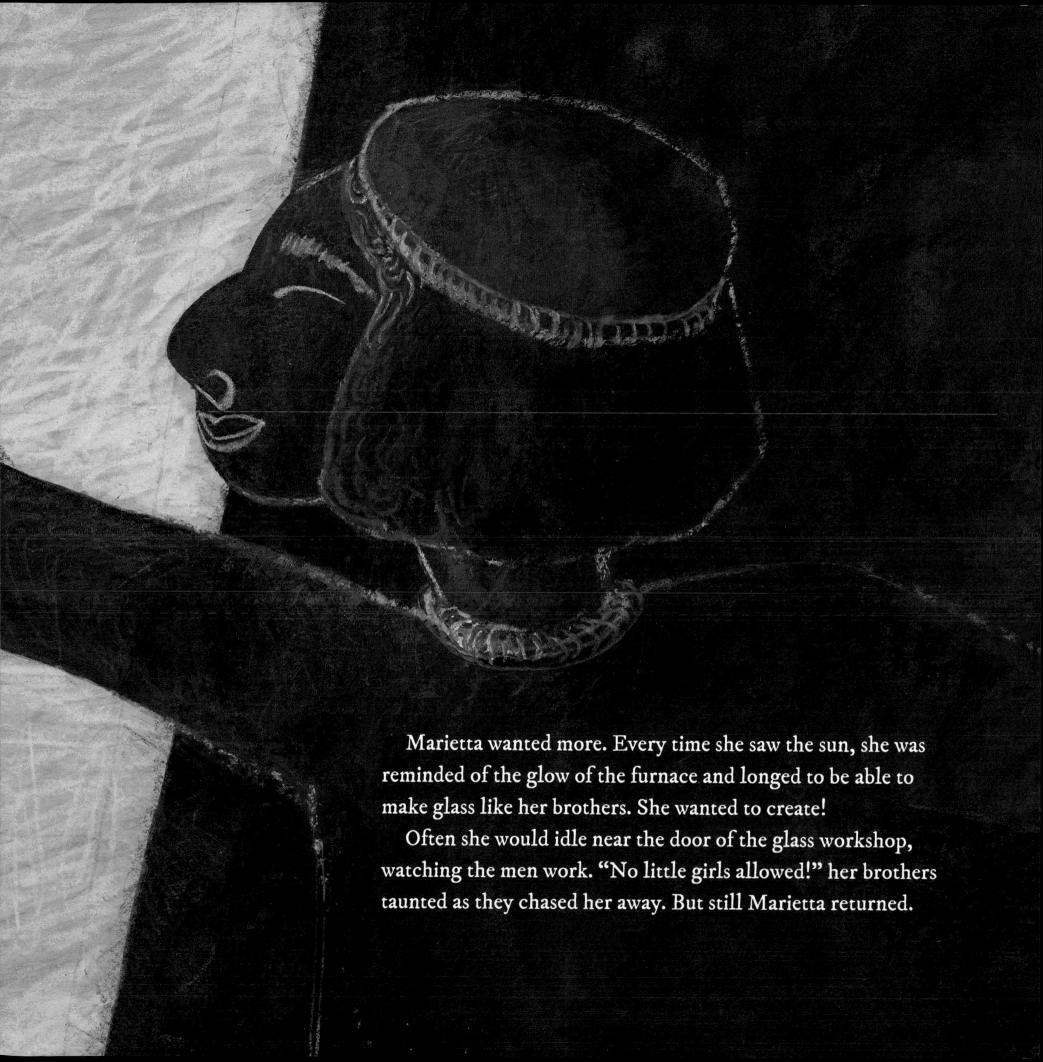

Marietta wanted more. Every time she saw the sun, she was reminded of the glow of the furnace and longed to be able to make glass like her brothers. She wanted to create!

Often she would idle near the door of the glass workshop, watching the men work. "No little girls allowed!" her brothers taunted as they chased her away. But still Marietta returned.

One day, her father noticed her peeking and beckoned her inside. As Marietta stepped into the workshop for the first time, she felt the immense heat of the furnace engulf her. She stared into the blinding light of the *bocca,* the mouth, of the furnace as her father gathered glass onto a long iron blowpipe.

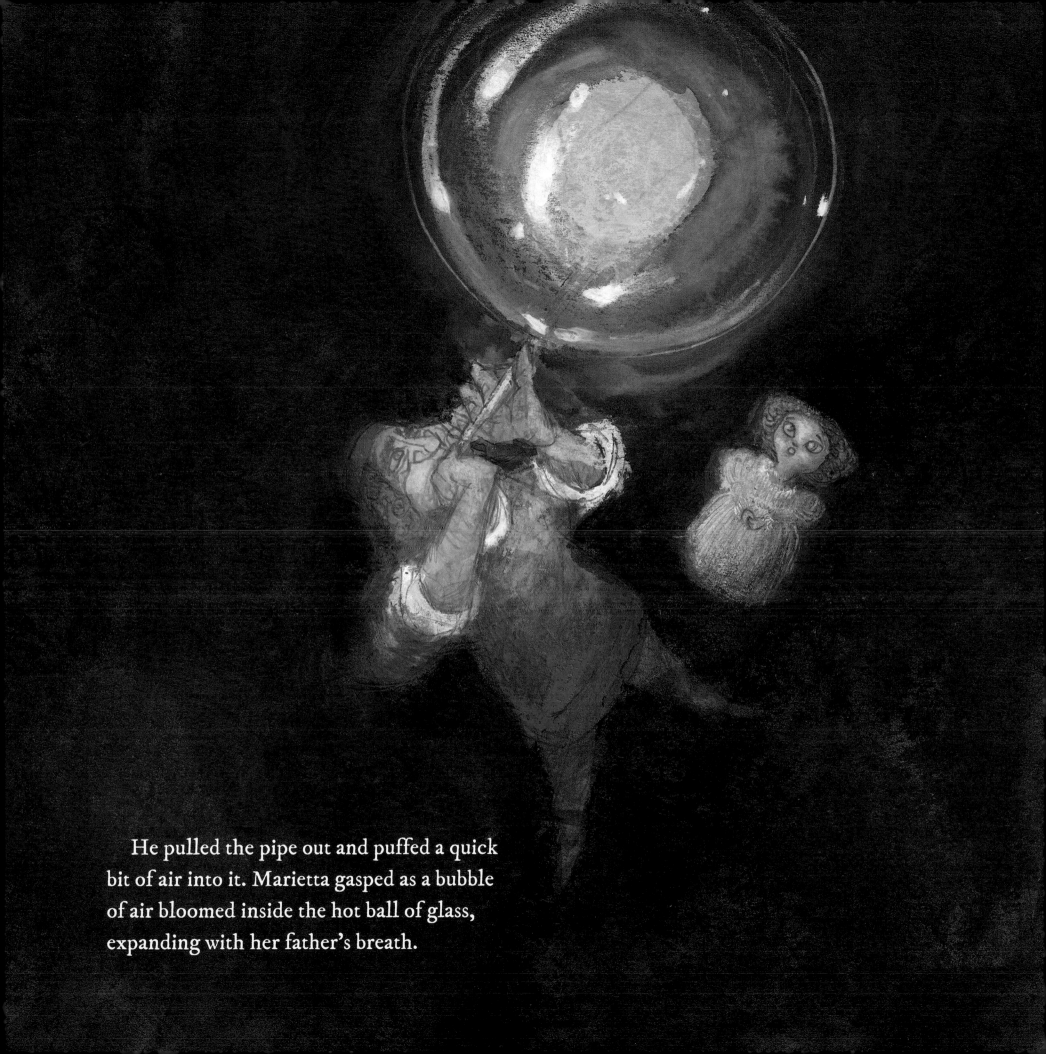

He pulled the pipe out and puffed a quick
bit of air into it. Marietta gasped as a bubble
of air bloomed inside the hot ball of glass,
expanding with her father's breath.

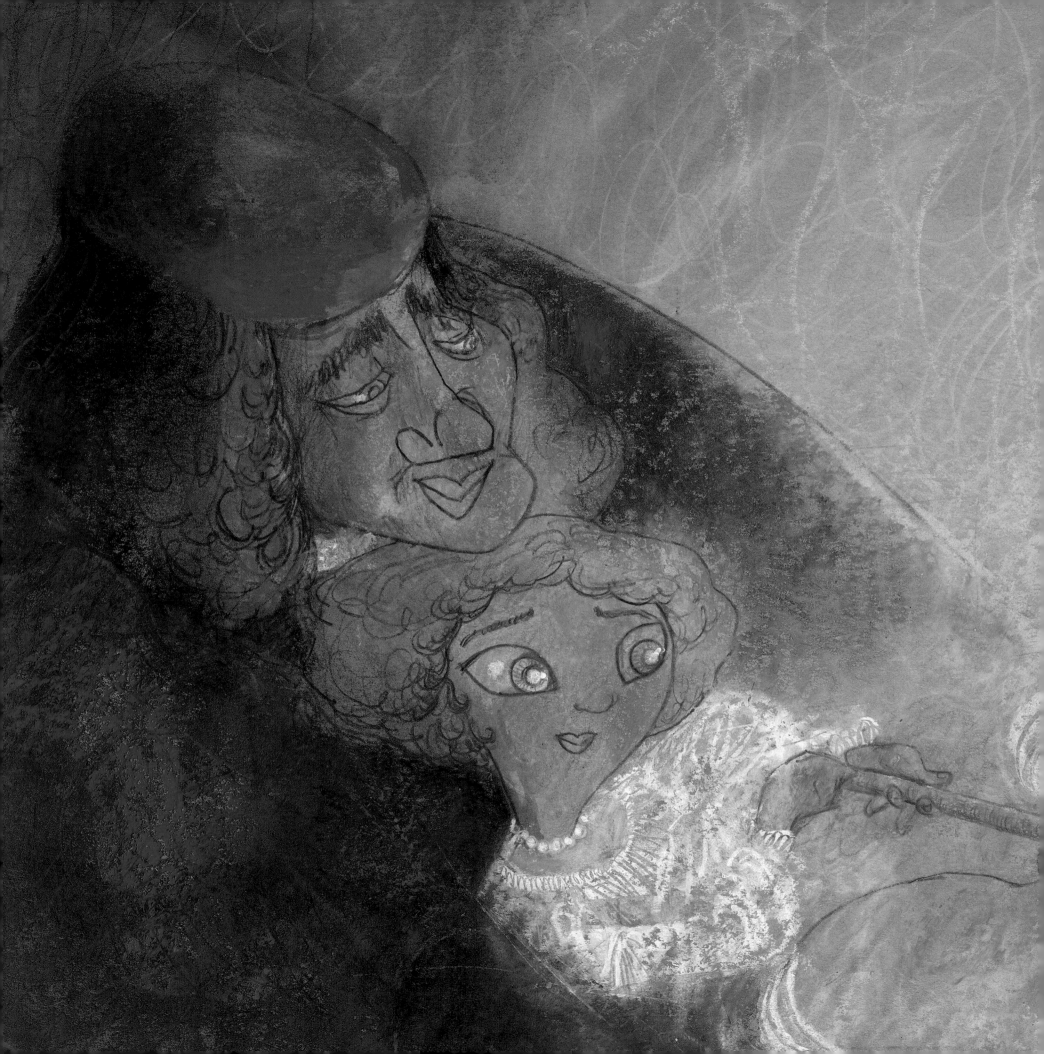

Her father smiled. "Now you, my dear."
Gently he held her hands on the pipe as he
twirled it, guiding it toward the furnace.
A rush of heat and light and fear hit her.
Her skin must surely be on fire! She struggled
to see as her father dipped the pipe to swirl
the glass onto the end. He lifted the pipe out
and began to blow again.

Marietta felt raw and red from the heat.
Even the sun could not be this bright or this
hot. In stunned silence she watched as her
father continued to perform his miracles.

Marietta awoke the next morning still blinking away the image of the furnace, but it would not disappear. Gingerly she touched the red skin on her palm and felt a tingle of fear return. But along with it came a wave of exhilaration and purpose.

She returned to her father's door.

Once again he smiled and brought her inside. The heat was just as intense as before. Marietta hesitated, but then she heard one of her brothers laugh. She stood a little taller and walked over to stand beside her father near the furnace. Marietta pushed her fear away and moved her pipe closer to the *bocca*.

The blaze of heat nearly knocked her over, but she made sure her hands didn't shake. Steadily she guided the pipe, twirling it as her father had shown her, and watched the molten glass swirl around the tip. At last she pulled the pipe out and admired the tiny ball of glass she had collected. The boys stopped giggling.

Marietta felt her dreams begin to take shape, and from then on, her father often taught her and let her observe. The heat of the furnace no longer frightened her. When it came to business, though, her brothers came first.

"Today I go with Father to Venice!" her older brother Marino bragged.

"Take me with you!" she pleaded as he closed the door behind him. Day after day she watched them leave for places she thought she would never see.

Early one morning, her father entered her room with a grin.

"*Cara* Marietta, today you will accompany me to Venice.
A wealthy patron has asked me to create a work of glass for him."

Marietta beamed.

She and her father boarded an ornate gilded *gondola* at
the dock, and the *gondoliere* paddled them through the early
morning fog to Venice.

They passed under bridge after bridge until they arrived at the Grand Canal. Hundreds of *gondole* slid by in every direction, full of travelers, merchants, nobles, and fishermen. Their *gondola* stopped in front of the most brilliantly gleaming palace Marietta could have imagined.

Her father's patron led them into a room filled with grand pedestals, each topped with a beautiful piece of glass. One in particular caught Marietta's eye. It was not the biggest, or the showiest, but it was unique. It was a small bowl, not much bigger than the palm of her hand, which looked like it had a field of flowers forever blooming across its surface.

Marietta was entranced. "That, my dear, is very old," the patron said. "Alas, the technique has been lost for hundreds of years. That's part of what makes this piece so special."

As they left, Marietta wished this magical day would never end. Then her father winked and whispered something to the *gondoliere*, who continued farther down the Grand Canal to the most exquisite building Marietta had ever seen.

"This is San Marco, and these incredible pictures are made with tiny pieces of glass and stone called *tessere*," her father whispered. "We call them *mosaici*, mosaics."

Marietta gaped at the twinkling golden scenes, shimmering with millions of individual pieces. She had never seen something so tiny become part of something so grand. Marietta imagined herself as one of the glittering tiles, yearning to see what dazzling picture she was to help create.

As time passed, Marietta's skills grew and grew. She was never happier than when she was in the heat of the furnace. Finally her brothers saw what she could do. When their father passed on, he left his workshop in the capable hands of his children, and to Marietta he entrusted his precious recipes for colored glass. Many in Murano laughed at the idea of a woman doing a man's job, and some of the other glassmakers even conspired against her.
But Marietta kept working.

The years went on, and as Marietta worked, memories of her childhood would often drift across her mind. She cherished each one like a precious jewel. One day, as she stared into the furnace, she gasped as an idea began to glow in her mind.

She remembered the immense, glittering mosaics of San Marco, made up of pieces so small yet so eternal, as she gathered white glass from the hot sun of the furnace.

She remembered the ever-blooming flowers of the ancient bowl as she filled the glass with her breath.

She remembered how her father had made miracles with glass and opened her eyes to the wonder of creating. She dipped the glass into layer after layer of brilliant red, white, and blue glass, pressing it into a star-shaped mold each time.

She remembered the heat of the furnace, and the fear she had once felt.

She remembered all those who had laughed at her.

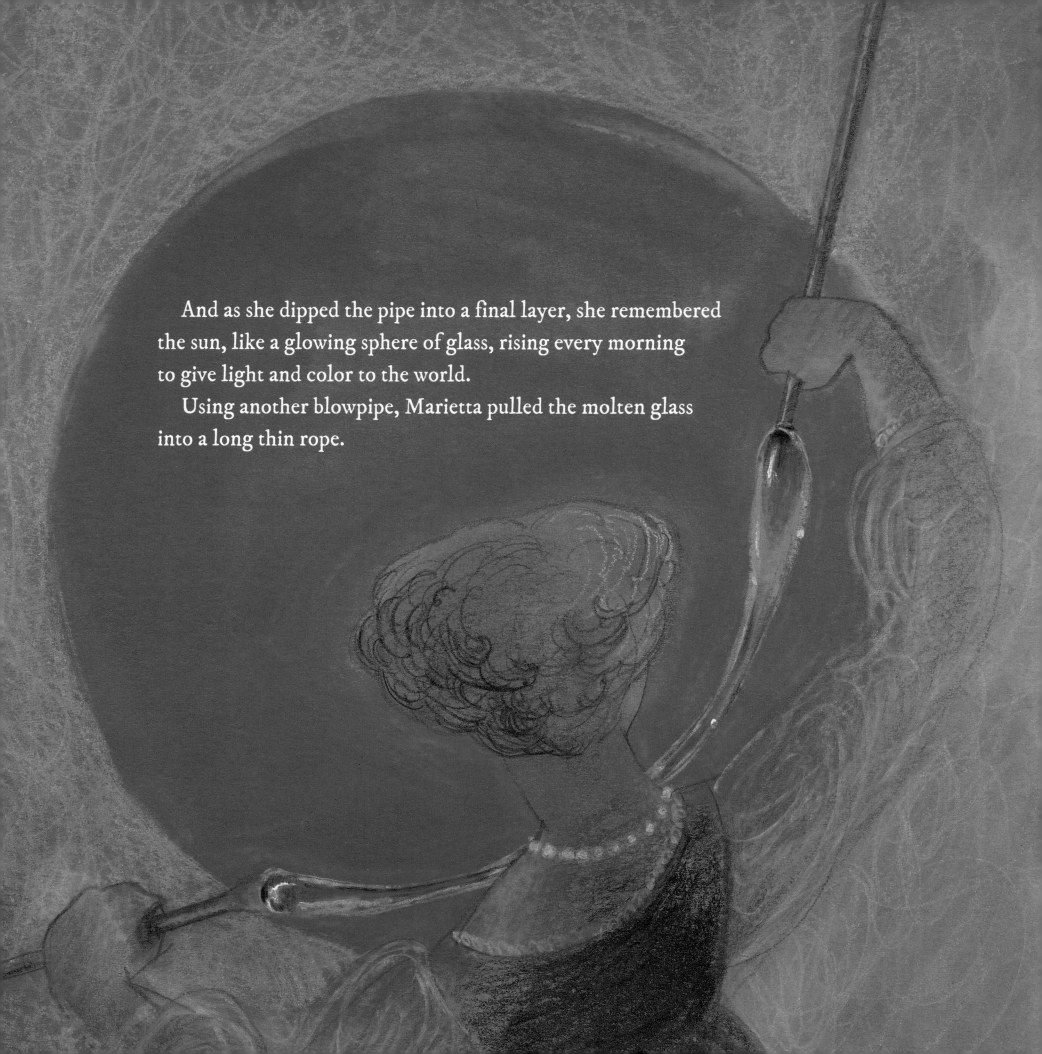

And as she dipped the pipe into a final layer, she remembered the sun, like a glowing sphere of glass, rising every morning to give light and color to the world.

Using another blowpipe, Marietta pulled the molten glass into a long thin rope.

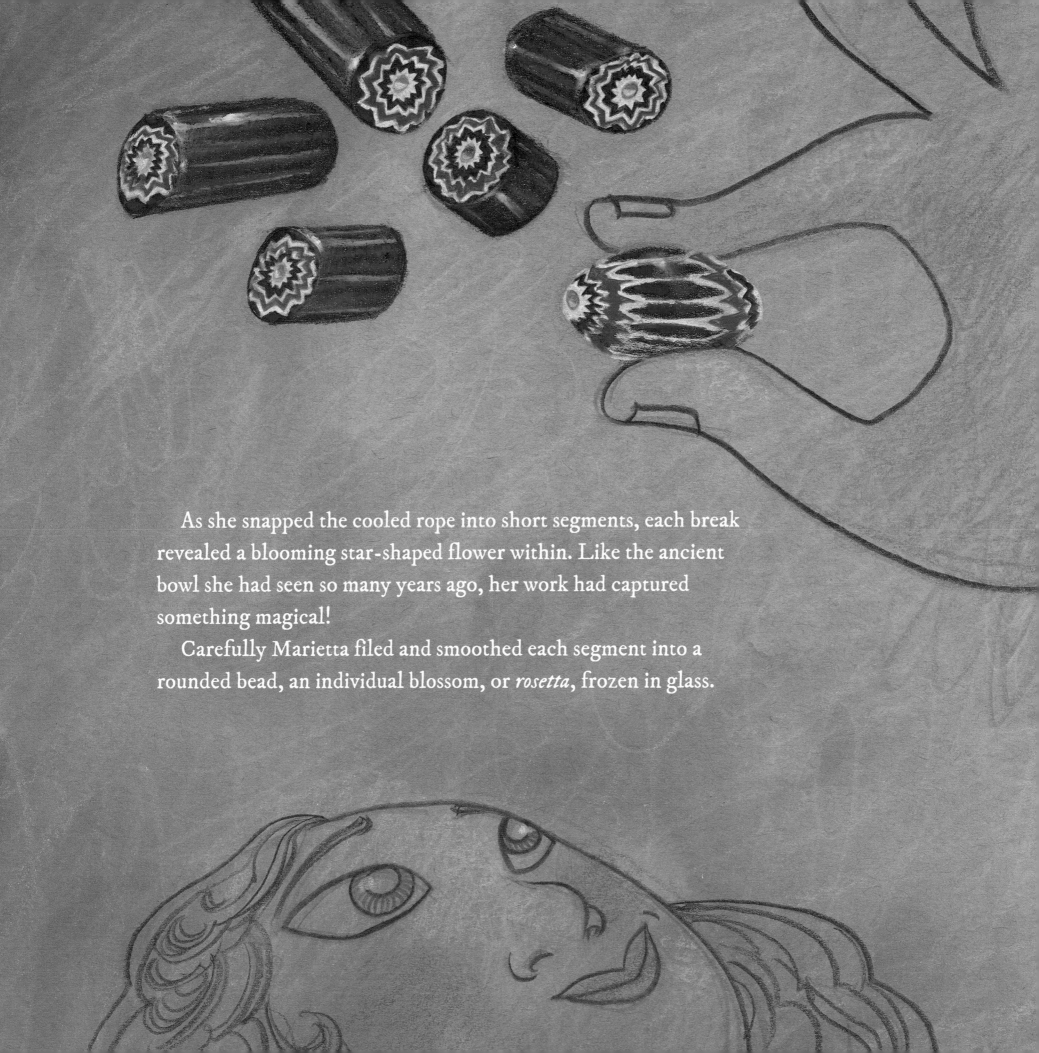

As she snapped the cooled rope into short segments, each break revealed a blooming star-shaped flower within. Like the ancient bowl she had seen so many years ago, her work had captured something magical!

Carefully Marietta filed and smoothed each segment into a rounded bead, an individual blossom, or *rosetta*, frozen in glass.

One by one she strung them into a necklace, each bead
a memory opened at the center with the breath she had given.

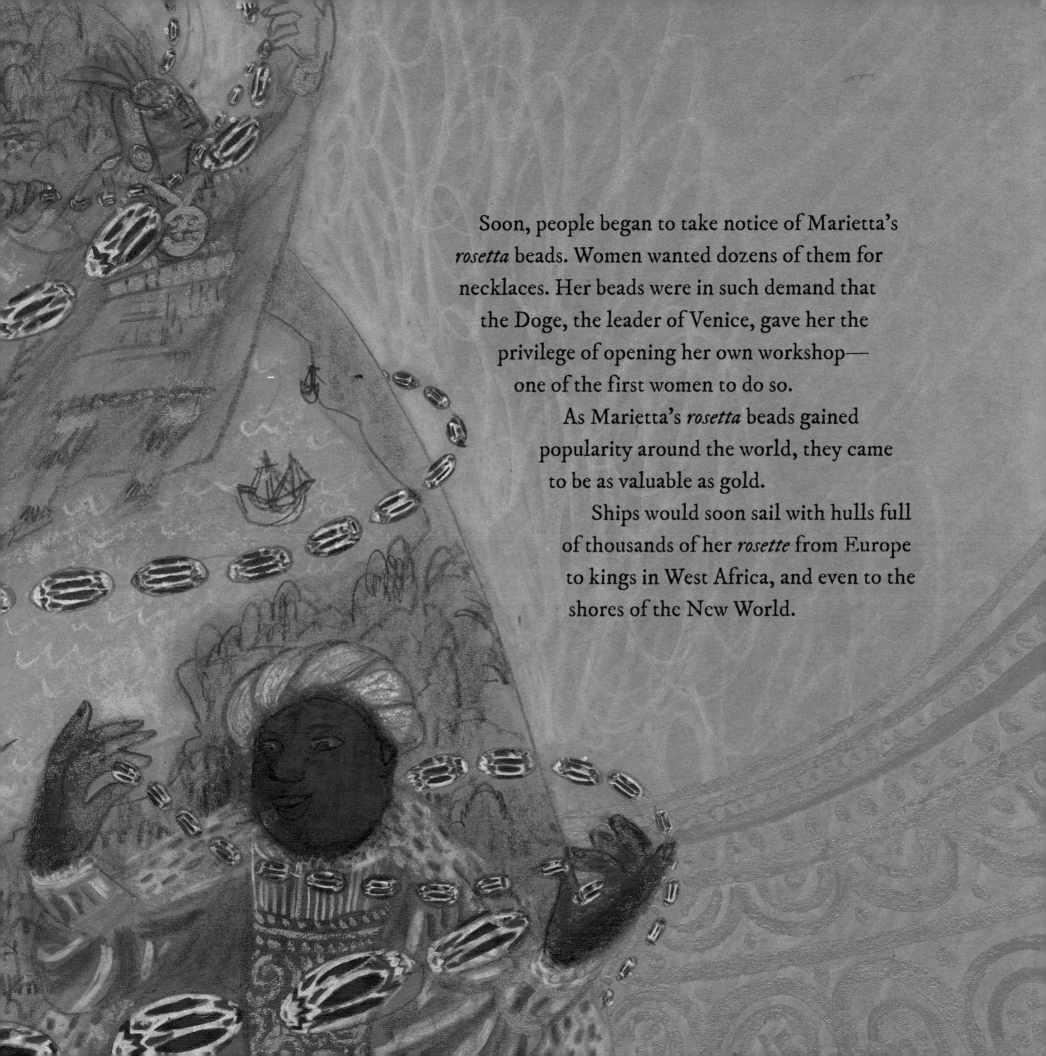

Soon, people began to take notice of Marietta's *rosetta* beads. Women wanted dozens of them for necklaces. Her beads were in such demand that the Doge, the leader of Venice, gave her the privilege of opening her own workshop— one of the first women to do so.

As Marietta's *rosetta* beads gained popularity around the world, they came to be as valuable as gold.

Ships would soon sail with hulls full of thousands of her *rosette* from Europe to kings in West Africa, and even to the shores of the New World.

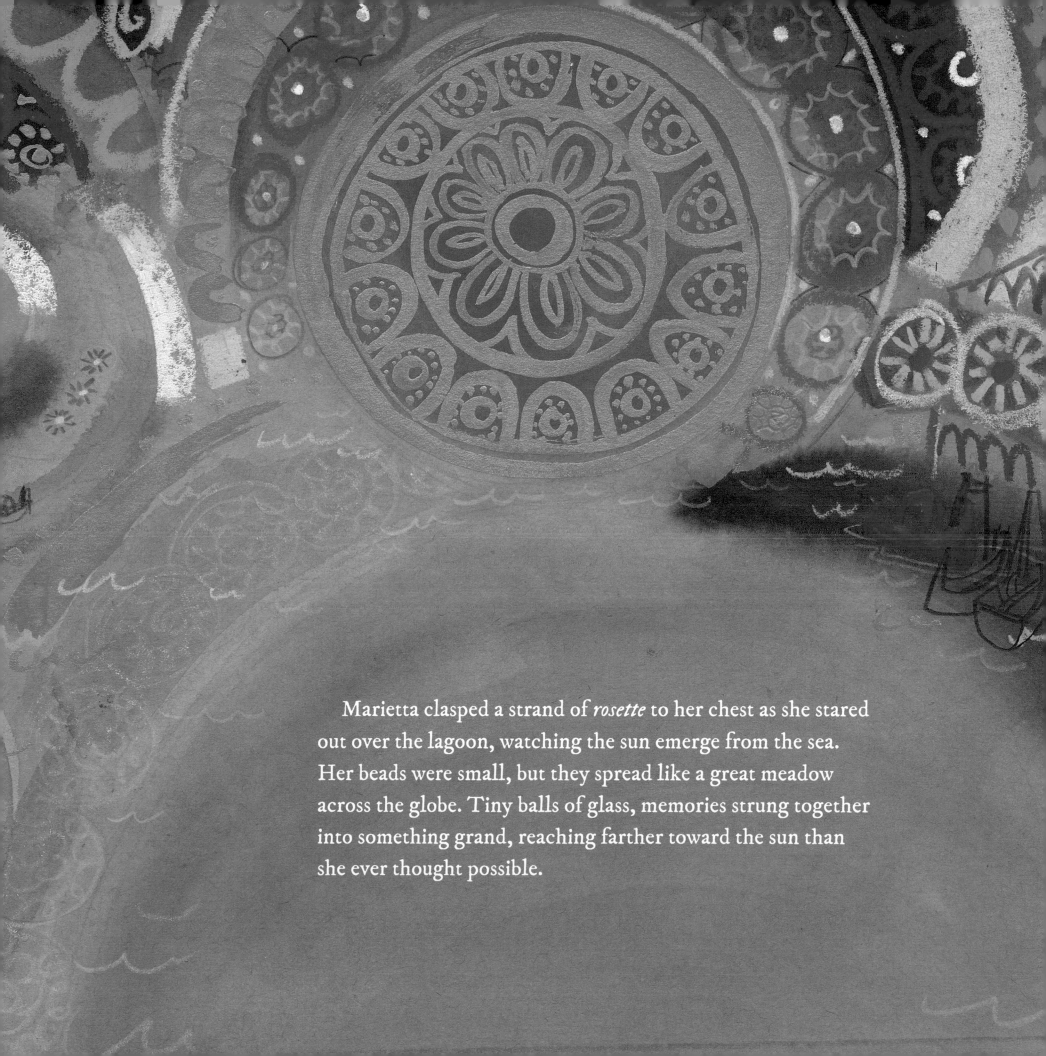

Marietta clasped a strand of *rosette* to her chest as she stared out over the lagoon, watching the sun emerge from the sea. Her beads were small, but they spread like a great meadow across the globe. Tiny balls of glass, memories strung together into something grand, reaching farther toward the sun than she ever thought possible.

Author's Note

"*Millefiori*," meaning "a thousand flowers" in Italian, is the modern name for the type of glass that Marietta (Maria) Barovier rediscovered through her creation of the *rosetta* bead. The beads are made from segments cut from long ropes of layered glass called "canes." The technique has existed for thousands of years, first in Egypt, then later in Rome. The oldest examples are made of fused glass (like the bowl Marietta observed in the story), where the segments of cane were put into a mold and heated until they fused together. With the fall of the Roman Empire, the technique was lost for hundreds of years until it was rediscovered in the late fifteenth century. The first documentation of its return was the *rosetta* bead in the glassworks inventory of Marietta and her brother Giovanni from 1496. The following year, the Doge of Venice granted Marietta permission to open her own furnace, becoming one of the first women ever allowed to do so. Her furnace was for making small glass items that scholars believe to have been the *rosetta* beads. In the eighteenth century, millefiori had another resurgence, and it became globally famous as a symbol of Murano glass yet again.

The Baroviers are one of the oldest and most prominent glassmaking families in Murano's history, with records going back to at least 1310. For this book, I met with one of Marietta's relatives, Rosa Barovier Mentasti, who is a well-known glass historian in Venice. The company Barovier & Toso is still around today, and until recently was still family owned. Marietta's father, Angelo, is one of the most revered glassmakers in Venetian history, and is credited with the discovery of colorless clear glass, or *cristallo* (crystal). He also used his background in chemistry to develop recipes for white milk glass (*lattimo*), a swirling colorful glass called chalcedony that looks like stone, and many other intense colors. His recipes were carefully guarded secrets, protected from foreign spies by the Venetian government, and from other Murano glassmakers trying to copy his techniques.

When Angelo died, Marietta and her brothers inherited his glassworks. Not much is known of Marietta's life, aside from the few times she was documented in historical records, so I invented much of this story around those pieces of history and speculating on how she might have arrived at her beautiful innovation. Her connection with her father was clear, though, through the fact that he left his most precious recipes for colored glass to her when he died. Glass scholar Luigi Zecchin believes that these recipes likely led to her creation of the vividly colored *rosetta* bead. To this day, glassblowing is still a heavily male-dominated industry, but there are now renowned female glass artists all over the world.

The *rosetta* bead attributed to Marietta Barovier went on to become one of the most valuable currencies of the Renaissance world. Ships sailed from the Netherlands to West Africa with thousands of the beads in their hulls, and West African kings traded gold, ivory, and enslaved people for the beads. Early Spanish conquistadores traded with glass beads upon landing in the Americas, and even Christopher Columbus is said to have paid for passage across the seas with a strand of *rosetta* beads.

Marietta Barovier grew up in a world that did not typically allow women to own businesses, or reward women who worked instead of married. The first documented mention of her was in 1431, in her mother's will, which set set aside sixty ducats (the Venetian currency of the time) for Marietta's eventual wedding. But there is no record of Marietta ever marrying or having children, and her legacy as an artist and artisan lives on through the global impact of the *rosetta* bead and the endurance of millefiori as a symbol of Venetian glass today.

About the Art

For this book, I wanted the art to capture the beauty and vibrancy of Venice, its lagoon, its architecture, and the brilliant feeling of light and color in Murano glass. I was able to go to Venice and Murano to experience it in person, and to draw and observe master glassmaker Davide Salvadore and talk with him about his work. I went to the Corning Museum of Glass in Corning, New York, where I made drawings of the incredible glassmaker and Renaissance glass historian William Gudenrath, to better understand the process. It truly is magical to see how the glowing, molten ball of glass is pulled, blown, and pushed into incredible shapes. Later, I even took a glass-blowing workshop in Corning to experience the process myself! Being so close to the heat of the furnace and feeling the difficulty and excitement of the process shaped how I imagined Marietta must have felt in that environment.

To try to capture the feeling of the time period in the art, I looked at Renaissance artists like Sandro Botticelli and Artemisia Gentileschi. I looked carefully at the paintings of Gentile Bellini and Vittore Carpaccio, who both made incredibly detailed paintings of Venice in Marietta's time, which serve as some of the only historical records of what Venice looked like in that era. To capture the feeling of color, light, and movement in the glass and water of Venice, I looked to Impressionist artists like Pierre Bonnard, Mary Cassatt, and Raoul Dufy. Impressionist painters often worked outdoors, using bright colors to capture changing light and emotion in a painting. I also looked at the art of Sonia Delaunay, who, although she was from a much later time (1885–1979), created work that felt just like the bright colors and dynamic energy of millefiori. I used a combination of bright watercolors, colored pencils, oil pastels, and gold gouache on tan paper to show the powerful dark and light contrast of the glass workshop and the amazing colors of Murano glass.

An enormous thank-you to William Gudenrath, Rosa Barovier Mentasti, Davide Salvadore, Yoshiko Tanimura, and Regan Brumagen for helping to make this book a reality.